DATE DUE		
~~OCT 14 2002~~ MAR 12 2010		

PRESENTATION PIECE

Presentation Piece

MARILYN HACKER

The Viking Press · New York

this book is for Chip, and for China

CONTENTS

PART THREE

PART FOUR

PRESEN
TATION
PIECE

Part One

Presentation Piece

About the skull of the beloved, filled
with unlikely innocence, liver pâté,
tidbits in aspic. You were never
anybody's "lover," should live
in staterooms full of temporary homage.
The corridor slants, cradled on the
crest of an
earthquake. Far above, smokestacks
proceed through badlands of snapped bridges.

About the skull of the beloved, filled
with a perilous remedy, sloshing
into the corners of the damp eyes
where you are reflected, twice, upside
down. The last image before
death is recorded photographically
on the retina for half an hour.
Prints can be made. The darkroom
is at the end of the corridor.

"These are worlds that were his thighs." You are
the assistant purser, translating
and filing telegraphic messages. "Arriving
Thursday 2 PM." "Take another little
piece of my heart now baby." "Armed and awaiting
signal before tides change." One of the messages

may be for you. "In an affluent society
cannibalism
is a sexual predilection."

That is not fresh meat. It was kept overnight
in a tub of brine. Hand remembers
the ribs' wet parting, the heavy pulse on the palm.
This is not the door to the engine room
though a pulse whines in the walls.
Green velvet ropes enlace a green
velvet chaise-longue, beneath
the purple jewels of the parvenu
empress. Meet me tonight under your tongue.

There is no easy way up. Bite
on your lip; do you taste what I do?
A gold skewer
pierces and joins his hands; the handle
is a five-leafed rose. Let me live
in your mouth; I know a place
where the earlobe is imperfectly joined to the skull.
At sunrise
we can look across the wasted sea for miles.

Learning Distances
for William McNeill

I

Snapdragons in a sandy teapot,
green pepper mottled vermilion
in a fluted white dish.
A film of distances over the yellow-gray
morning. The houseplants murmur. The cat sleeps.
Set on wood, the artifacts of friendship order time.
So much stops in the window.
Leaves etched on light. Who are these trees?
                                        My mother
grew marigolds rimming the retaining wall,
spindly, hard, bright.
                        The trees soak morning
with a smell of alarm and cut leaves.

This is as real as any other language:
your jawbone buttressed by your hand,
a mouth falling to speech through gravity,
the stretch between the corners of my eyes.
Words through wires are
bitter between tongue and palate,
between thumb and forefinger,
abrasion of an undrawn chart.

I could tell you, change moves in the moment.
I could tell you, plant grass in your open palm.
I could tell you, take the chains of a white room,

sit in the prison of a windowpane,
close your hands on pebbled granite hours.
This is as real as any other language.

II

It is a privilege to learn a language,
a journey into the immediate
morning, leaf yellow
filtering the white sill,
shaping the building outside,
the place of human wonder in a structure,
the living figure in the windowpane,
the invocation of the possible
moment demanding this motion:
perception,
placement,
praise.

Each time it is necessary
to relearn the entire
process, not to remember but
re-enter the wrench
of seconds on contracted
muscles, the foam tingling
capillaries, that pulse
beating that vision
on the turn of the light-shot
river, below the double height
mahogany lintel, under the ecru
stucco spilling dawn.

I crushed privet leaves
for the green sap and bitter smell
and learned on broken weeds
the pain of fire and water
which is as real as any other
language.

Chanson de l'enfant prodigue

The child of wonder looks in bed
at naked ceilings overhead.
Infinity eats up the skies
as burning teardrops cauterize
his wet white eyes.

The child of wonder cannot pass
the curved rococo looking-glass.
Suspended in between the pair,
body and image frozen there,
he whirls to stare.

The child of wonder, deep in his
gut, knows how long forever is,
and, like a haunted anarchist,
hears a repeated order hissed
not to exist.

The child of wonder juggles word
and number; he has often heard
that theorem is not destroyed
and song, peculiarly employed,
endures a void.

The child of wonder lies alone
and touch or thought ignites the bone
and thrills the flesh. But through the grate

he hears the wind come, insensate,
to annihilate.

The child of wonder watches day
arrive. Premature dawn is gray
and flat upon the wet earth he
perceives intangibility
and is not free.

An Alexandrite Pendant for My Mother

I am not in my country, and my home
shifts in the prism of a purple stone
looped round by slender golden straits. Within,
a fist of windy palm-swards clashes, bends
behind the gray ephemera of rain.
Another night. Dogs bark against the dawn.

The traveler awakens before dawn,
yawns, and shakes off a troubled dream of home.
The stray dogs in the street shake off the rain,
shelter themselves behind a jutting stone,
under a porch; the rooted conscience bends,
evades the drenching distances within.

A window lights, ochers the court. Within,
the shadow of a schoolgirl greets the dawn
with drowsy knees and elbows. Then she bends
and draws the shade, a child's ferocious home
closed round her like a carapace of stone,
rejecting ripe and rot into the rain.

This city is emprismed in the rain.
Echoes rise with morning from within
the courtyard, walled with tile and porous stone;
the maids, kneeling at zinc washtubs since dawn,
sing of men riding, women kept at home
vigilant where the mountain roadway bends.

Vigilant as exile, now I bend
over the mirror of blue tiles and rain
whose silence is the only lasting home,
having no voice to call the streets with. In
another city, nightwalkers watch dawn
break blue on river wharf and pavingstone.

This is an island city, propped on stone,
whose roots are swamp, whose tallest tower bends
when trembling earth shatters to a new dawn;
as when, across the lake, glimpsed through the rain,
serpent and eagle coupled signs within
the glyph of death where warriors make their home.

Mother of exiles, home of enduring stone
within the glimpsed point where the road bends,
rain fortune on my voyaging this dawn.

The Dark Twin

                              turning in the brain, to wake
with wires behind his eyes, forking the joints
akimbo. He wakes, wired,
forked fingers crackling, gagging on his tongue.
We wake, turning.
                              Spined against the floor,
his spine turning, chest hollowed,
air in the wires, sparks
glinting from the wired ceiling, tapping
his sparking fingernails. Coughs, cries.
The dark twin doubles on the floor, swallows his tongue.
Splashed to the dark pole circuited behind
the eyes, the dark twin snaps his spine free, slaps
his palms against the ceiling. Charged beads fly.
The ceiling, polarized, batters his cheek with metal.
Tears free skin. Tears ribs,
torn pectorals off metal curved away
black, behind the cracks, dried,
that are his torn lips. More.
Buttocks and shoulderblades grind on the floor
gritty and green with brine.
                              They wake.
We wake, turning.
                              He, gargling blood, turns,
born, on the wet floor.
The dark twin turns in the brain. We wake.

From *The Old Reliable*

We draw inland for the winter. Skies
are cannonmetal with a smell of snow.
Through the bar the mohair fairies go
with rum-and-cokes and big cosmetic flies.
A young Italian cop sits near the door
smudging his record-book with woolen sleeves.
He turns and scowls when anybody leaves.
It isn't too effective any more.
Over brandy and between the queens
chilled poets plan fantastic magazines
while trapezoidal Margie at the bar
intuits profit on the way things are
and lifts a steaming glass of Russian tea
to winter outcasts on her property.

Exiles

Her brown falcon perches above the sink
as steaming water forks over my hands.
Below the wrists they shrivel and turn pink.
I am in exile in my own land.

Her half-grown cats scuffle across the floor
trailing a slime of blood from where they fed.
I lock the door. They claw under the door.
I am in exile in my own bed.

Her spotted mongrel, bristling with red mange,
sleeps on the threshold of the Third Street bar
where I drink brandy as the couples change.
I am in exile where my neighbors are.

On the pavement, cans of ashes burn.
Her green lizard scuttles from the light
around torn cardboard charred to glowing fern.
I am in exile in my own sight.

Her blond child sits on the stoop when I
come back at night. Cold hands, blue lids; we both
need sleep. She tells me she is going to die.
I am in exile in my own youth.

Lady of distances, this fire, this water,
this earth make sanctuary where I stand.
Call off your animals and your blond daughter.
I am in exile in my own hands.

She Bitches about Boys

To live on charm, one must be courteous.
To live on others' love, one must be lovable.
Some get away with murder being beautiful.

Girls love a sick child or a healthy animal.
A man who's both itches them like an incubus,
but I, for one, have had a bellyful

of giving reassurances and obvious
advice with scrambled eggs and cereal;
then bad debts, broken dates, and lecherous

onanistic dreams of estival
nights when some high-strung, well-hung, penurious
boy, not knowing what he'd get, could be more generous.

The Navigators

Between us on our wide bed we cuddle an incubus
whom we have filled with voyages. We wake
more apart than before, with open hands.
Your stomach and my head begin to ache.
We cannot work. You are in pain. I cry.
Outside the dirty window, in the damp
film of new spring, muddy brown children dabble
cardboard in puddles, chalk across a wall
where two boys on a fire-escape eat oranges.
Love, longing makes us both anonymous,
middle-aged, quarrelsome, ridiculous.
You hurt for want of tears. I cry for pain.

Real, grimy and exiled, he
eludes us.
I would show him books and bridges,
and make a language we could all speak.

No blond fantasy
Mother has sent to plague us in the spring,
he has his own bad dreams, needs work, gets drunk,
maybe would not have chosen to be beautiful.

Because we held him while he screamed or threw up,
were good in bed, or good for a hot meal,
we were not given his life by the scruff of its neck | 17

or even the right to speak too much out of turn.
Love, my love, is not what you have done
but what you are just now doing.

Oh, I would hold his head and feed him oranges
to taste his warm home,
pink shrimp to taste the green lick of the sea.
To taste the road, tart, cold wild apples
and long pale grapes with dusty moon skins.
To taste my love, amber Greek honey
that coats his tongue with sweet thinking of bitter.
To taste my love, raw meat, radishes, lemons
and salt rubbing his lips where they are broken.

II

I spread his callused hand like a closed plant.
Machines and ropes ripped scars across his palm
leaving it tough and skillful. Watching him wake
or read or take my camera apart,
I learn what learning is and how the eye
reverses image into memory.
Have I learned his face in this much time,
grotesque with concentration, creased with sleep,
the fear that grays his eyes at a knocked door,
the angle of his chin when he is lying?
Levi'd, blond and greasestained, the American Dream
cannot love the Jew's devious daughter.
He shrugs her spells off adolescent shoulders.
She cannot witch him with her ancient language
or scraps of denim sleeve under her pillow,
or comb his name in her long hair with ivory.
He never knows whose son he is, and she
would not be other than her Mother's daughter.
Still, for a short while, we shed our myths
like spring skins and sat across a table,
over dark wood laboriously translated
till we, precarious, unique and human,
with naked hands and eyes, spoke to each other,
and something freer than necessity
tangled our arms and backs, merged our blue mornings.

III
You made an algebra: his tastes in food,
when the dinner guests would be too much
for him to keep his poise, his surly moods;
to calculate how often you could touch
the real boy like your dream sharing our bed,
one arm sprawled off the mattress near your head.
He slept. Your hands relaxed around his chest,
and all the ambiguities could rest
between your shoulder and his shoulderblades.
I saw you move your mouth against his nape,
wanting to wake him in your arms, afraid
of how his face would age coming awake.

IV

His Wife at Bellevue

Trackless and lost between piss-colored walls,
she huddles on the bench arm, hides her face,
shakes with sobs or dry retching. The intern calls
names in a bored voice. People shift in place.
Clocks sweep toward morning and she hides her face.
Between the red felt collar and her hair,
her neck is cracked with white beneath the brown.
I draw an old man. Three boys turn to stare
over their bench to see what I have down;
one has a bloody gash beneath his hair.
I am a stranger whom she cannot trust.
She hid her face and let me bring her here.
My hand quiets her trembling. Since she must
feel some hand on her sickness and her fear,
my hand is on her shoulder; we are here.

V

Across the mud flats and the wide roads, over rivers and
        borders,
by bus, truck, trailer, car and foot,
my two loves have gone, the dark and the fair.
Truck drivers, salesmen, schoolgirls on vacation
taste the salt fruit of their bodies.
They breathe strange air; strange hands press their
        shoulders,
strange voices speak to them.
Mother of exiles, save them from wind and rage.
Mother of journeys, let the sea be kind to them.

Along the highway, despair and dead animals
steam on the macadam. Sheet-white, the sky
closes them in. Miles apart, in a mud-wide state,
they sing out loud, and the long road is empty
from red hill to scrub-bush. Branches are bare with heat
and it's only May. Home and the ports
swing like a compass-needle, both far away.
Mother of exiles, save them from wind and rage.
Mother of journeys, let the sea be kind to them.

Together, briefly, they sit on splintered pilings.
Thick, spit-yellow foam slaps the Diesel hulls.
Storms are in the Gulf; the catch is north.

North on an old coast, landlocked on my island
dry in soot-thick summer, I spin their warmth.
I loop their names in words. One road is closed
to women and conspirators. I plot. I sing.
Mother of exiles, save them from wind and rage.
Mother of journeys, let the sea be kind to them.

VI

When you told me that he was in jail
again, I scrounged two hundred for his bail
in two hours, wired it down, came home, threw up,
cried while you brewed me coffee, and threw up,
and threw up every thirty minutes flat
for two days, till the airline ended that
and flew him back. Pale, tired, clean,
I took the Carey bus at two-fifteen
and waited at the terminal for him.
He had new, checked, pegged slacks. They'd cropped his
      hair.
He said he was surprised that I was there
and had I dieted to get so thin.
He asked why you weren't there, and I said, well,
you were engaging in diplomacy
and would be waiting up at the hotel;
which meant, you had to wait around and see
his wife. We took the bus back. It was dark
inside, but floodlit girders looped the park.
Grained, heavy cones of light spilled on the sky
as planes dropped to their runways through the mist.
There was a groan of engines as we kissed
and searchlights limned my hand over his thigh.

Seventy-Second Street; so tired it hurt.
The florid Slav bursting his dirty shirt
could see from the cash window what we were,
a trio of unluggaged travelers
wanting cheap beds and anonymity.
You signed for two, although he could see three.
Two bulldykes teased an acrid teenage whore
pinioned with dexies to the lobby door
and wondered if distinction could be made
among us, who was trick and who was trade.

The walls were hotel green. Someone had drawn
blue crayon mountains facing the iron bed.
We shelved our change of underwear. I yawned.
A swish of cars, a whiff of the dried dead
came through the blinded courtyard to the halls.
You went away that night. The tangled sheets
were heaped and ribboned underneath our feet.
I held him combed in foreign sounds. Thin walls
enclose nocturnal lexicons. He dreamed
of walls, baked concrete glaring at the sun.
Thick sewage sucked his chest. A milky gleam
slid on the trustee's buttons, and the gun-
barrel cocked on his hip swelled twice its size.
(I ground my fists in pillows, reading him.)
He threw his hands up to protect his eyes
and woke knocking his elbow on my chin.

VII

Bailed out too soon, back in our den of exiles,
he dreams of ships and speaks to us in code.
He hides his golden back from the June sun,
learns music from you, teaches me prisoners' games,
reads novels about glorious escapes.
Freedom is fugue, and love is a disease
the way they teach blond boys in Gulf port towns.
He is too sullen and too beautiful.
Deafened by music and his longing silence,
my mouth and hands no longer speak for me.
Writing, my fingers brush, and rub on him.
Talking, my tongue hits salt, and tastes him.
Then, where he was, an empty space and dreams,
the clean sea and his naked body, gold
in a spray of sun, round hard arms sweat oiled
reaching to fold me in. Between his hands
I wake; we, loving him, new strangers, wake.

VIII

A knot of journeys underneath my ribs
bursts like coming when an oilboat prow
slices the river night southward to sea
while humpbacked tugs chug north with open doors
between the hawsepipe flushing and the stalk
where two lights flash for barges. I will go
north on the coastal shuttle to the Keys
or southwest, over the border, across the mesas
down the devious flanks of red clay mountains
to the plaza lights of another city.
Amidst these exiles, I on my own ground
am exiled. I know the joy of journeys,
drowsing through dawn on a humming bus
rushing northeast, someone asleep on my shoulder;
woke with the palms of leaves pressed on the windows
in a coastal forest, smelling the sea;
crossed foreign mountains in a stranger's car
fleeing the unbelievable police
on the same ocean, thousands of miles south.
Distance is sometimes bitter in my mouth
but always spiced with something to be sought
or seen ahead, the sea again, the green
of ancient stone, old trees on a new sky,
the gaslight of a plaza, Spanish tile
chilling my bare feet, spiced tripe on my tongue

with onions in the morning.
This round exuberance could conquer art.
The air spins with adventures, and I spring
on my new body, letting them reach me
and catching open-handed. Air recoils
beneath my soles. Blue sky, scarred concrete
are walls to bounce off, grips to stretch and reach.
I hit the ground like live waves on a beach.

IX

My old city sinks to river winter.
Immobile and alone, I learn to lie
at desks, drink brandy, know my age,
digest somebody's overwritten page,
and love can't turn my stomach any more.
I vomited some bile, and I survive
with guts gone rational to stay alive.
Say if my hands are fit for making charts
that have been idle in their older arts.
Winter and age; we three are in our harbors
trying to make a basin of the sea
to bathe our hands together in, all three
sharing water over depths and miles
and losing touch in distance, speech in style.

X
Orpheus and animus,
drawing back to journeys now,
leaving me on shores behind
streets and shutters of the mind
as a new October streaks
dry hollows underneath our cheeks:
All that I have learned from you,
all that I have failed to learn,
I will order up again
with an overcautious pen,
making models, giving names
(nothing ever stays the same),
initiate the change that moves
the peripheries of love.

Part Two

Concordances

for Joanne Kyger

*State of a present
alphabetical index
of all the words
in a text*

I

Although I draw the philodendron
its leaves yellow and die; although
I draw the fringy coleus
it drops branches in first-freeze tantrums.
My walls are covered with growing plants
that died of cold and parasites.
So that isn't what it's for.

II
"The transverse beams that hold the snow," he said,
"darken the women's long days with eaved shadows,"
aware, amidst these rocks, that architecture
breathes in elemental lives.
Invent the house around a court, invent the women
gossiping over the well-shaft, invent
the novel again.
Even the weight of a quartz-veined
garden stone in a closed palm
dropped to thigh height, lifted
to eye level, jerked back and thrown
blueprints machines in the mind.
We are creatures of structure.

III

It drops through levity and aspirations:
pun with a landscape drawn around it.
Can you define a bottle with your elbows
and why try? (wanting to pull it off
more than anything.) "That is *not*
one of *my* attributes." Disguised
as a long girl eating peanut buttter sandwiches,
winding her calves around the chair legs, she leans
forward, the gap of her black V-neck revealing
the rowed dugs of Ephesian Diana,
spurting equations and wine.

IV

A man and a boy in a dirt lot
adjoining the construction site,
the man in blue clothes like a uniform,
the boy, a pale child on a brown block,
in shorts and gray knee socks: they talk.
The wood fence screens them from the street.
The man rolls up his sleeves and hauls
a pick up from a pile, heaves at the ground,
the fence, then spares the fence. The boy sits on his jacket,
white knees folded against the dark.
Dusk connects them, blotting street and tools.

A man and a woman in a green room
across the street from the lot, sitting
at a small mahogany table, placed
behind a row of potted plants,
begonia, philodendron, lemon shrub,
watch the man talk to the boy.
Over a bowl of greengages and figs
smoke hangs on the visible wind.
Between pictures of other rooms, light filters west.

Cities

for Link

Wrapped in thick sweaters in the high cold room,
we lie, holding each other, on my bed
covered with drapes, saying the names of cities.
The tree in the yard is heavy with snow,
the house is still as a boat in morning,
and I taste Alexandria on your tongue.
You traveled on the bodies of your lovers
away from the madwoman with keys
who locked you in her bedroom.
Smashing a vase and a tray, hiding the knives,
purchased no passport from the humid walls
soaking up voices shrill with loss. Soiled organdy
covered windows out over a city
where they spoke one language under the trees
and mauve skies opening evening.
There was a word like a lozenge on your tongue
and words buzzing the height of the darkening room.
How old were you the first morning,
awake in nervous freedom in a stranger's bed,
thinking of monsoon rivers, sheeted snow
blowing over the domes of possible cities?
Now you have visited many cities.
You draw their figured maps over my tongue.
There, mannered wolves track children through the snow.
There, the outlaw poet in his room

looks from the rumpled table to the bed
stained by the glimmer of a backward morning.

But there was another map you hid with the knives
in the buzzing room, and all your clever lovers
will never find the key.

For Elektra

My father dies again in dreams, a twin.
She stands above his dying like a small
vulture in curlers, twisting her veined hands,
knowing he died before. Looselimbed in underwear,
he slips from indolence to agony
on a rumpled double bed. His round
face flattens with pain. I, overgrown,
watch and fall distant till the dark green wall
is tentative beneath my palm. I fill the window light.
He is my father and my father's twin,
dying again. She did not kill or save him
with her dry hands. She does not touch him now.
The screech of her nails on my cheek. I presume
too much in giving you my mother monster
rehashed in pincurls from a guilty dream
where she slaps my hand for taking cakes and cocks
on my plate and failing, failing.
I will speak to you. You are not my brother,
unmasked on the river path as I long for exile.
Those black figures on the snow, too simply
dark fingers on a white thigh, establish
the clean hierarchic myth.
                      Brothers and brothers
pass under, pass over, but I never had
a brother. Lustful shorthaired virgin
bitch borrows the voice and says,

"Your Mother is my mother. Dare."
How she bores me with her metaphors.
I would rather make love and poems than kill
my mother. "So would I. Have you done
flaunting your cunt and your pen in her face
when she's not looking? High above your bed,
like a lamppost with eyes, stern as a pay toilet,
she stands, waiting to be told off
and tolled out." Waiting to be told off,
Miss Bitch puts me to work for nothing
at being my own brother, with such sisters.

The King of Cups Reversed

The King of Cups reversed has agate eyes
looking away and a stern chin.
He empties out wealth and suggests
the Army for a year, construction gangs,
a handbook of calligraphy: hard change.
Cold cash sticks to the ribs. No more
boys before breakfast. Clean your plate;
eat what the cats won't. In the midst
of opulence, he indicates the light
of one lantern on a windy crag,
brooding where the Fool fell or flew away.

His colors are yellow and blue. His boots
track up and down on the ceiling. This
is a way to break through. The poem
is about itself, breaks on its lines
and curves over them. We used the cards
to comment, and they sang the Tarot Blues
from tacky triumph to four swords turned down.
Real death is an ordinary card,
a low number in the virile suit.
It doesn't turn up often
                              like the pain
of cold bright afternoons when swords
are the three walls of a heart with no door.
March is a bad month for archers. The King

is hoisted on the horns of goats and bulls
as the sun nudges the cards to balance.
Reversed, the King of Cups suspects he's mad,
which knocks determination on the chin
too square and long. He has had
houses on the cliff over the tossed sea
where circling birds whistled like blades.
Now on this fidgety island, he
hands out silks and portents, telling the same
visionary tale of hills and rivers
in the dubious traffic of the bay,
while fishy elegance shakes for the eyes
of damp beasts and the winged ape hidden in the tree.

Ruptured Friendships,
       or,
The High Cost of Keys

I am obliged to repossess
some nooks and crannies of my soul.
I do not think of you the less.

Tonight's ragout would be a mess
without the red clay casserole
I am obliged to repossess.

The green chair suits my dinner dress.
The silk throw makes a pretty stole. . . .
I do not think of you the less.

Six forks, two serving-spoons, and, yes,
a platter and a salad-bowl
I am obliged to repossess.

Indeed, I say, more courtliness
would land me quickly on the dole.
I do not think of you the less.

Malicious mischief? I confess
the quicker I forget that role
and do not think of you, the less
I am obliged to repossess.

Elektra on Third Avenue
for Link

At six, when April chills our hands and feet
walking downtown, we stop at Clancy's Bar
or Bickford's, where the part-time hustlers are,
scoffing between the mailroom and the street.
Old pensioners appraise them while they eat,
and so do we, debating half in jest
which piece of hasty pudding we'd like best.
I know you know I think your mouth is sweet
as anything exhibited for sale,
fresh coffee cake or boys fresh out of jail,
which tender hint of incest brings me near
to ordering more coffee or more beer.
The homebound crowd provides more youth to cruise.
We nurse our cups, nudge knees, and pick and choose.

Lines on the Death of Madame de Staël

When she lay, dropsical, myopic, dying,
exiled from Paris, harried across France,
they realized at last that she was trying
for something more than getting in their pants.
That old-boys' club of desultory lovers,
toothy and shrill, gathered around the bed
and watched the bloated aspic under covers,
with the carnivorous despotic head
carved down by loss of teeth and hair in fever
to a hooked relic of the Fisher King,
hawk order with an epigram, deliver
last cutting justice. The cathedral ring
reverberated from the walls, intact,
while strained and astigmatic eyes still looked
caroming after the last artifacts
of reign, that one mute boy, that one loud book.

Alba: August

One morning you woke me
kissing my shoulders
as the rooster on the next block crowed.
New light
blued in the window full of plants,
and the next-door crash pad
got Sergeant Pepper in the day's first groove.

Dancing
between moving limbs,
the slow flowers
of our friction opened
together. So quickly
you were salt and sweet
on my tongue, like the desert
we drove through, asleep
on each other's shoulders.

Alba: September

Orange plastic filters light
spilling on legs in sworls of sheets.
Sweet, your veiled eyes—I dreamed
you told me off beneath a monolith
in limestone, a cafe under a tower
where you and older poets drank vermouth-cassis,
and woke because your lover, holding you
diagonally on the bed, was shoving me
between the mattress and the wall, determinedly
asleep. Clever Jean-Paul imagined hell
unloving threesies in a cheap hotel.
No room in that bed. Your cock spills on your thigh
out of its black bush like some thorny fruit
I've been told not to touch. Sleep and don't smile
that crazy candlepower for a while
all for his blue eyes, and maybe I can sleep
a little. Yellow mornings keep.

Alba: October

Falling asleep or waking
my mouth is full of brine
like the taste of your skin.
You are in
another city, climbing
a hill that views the sea. Under
the fat light of bay
windows, shiny omnivorous
leaves crunch open for a wet
lunch. Born
in a city without
seasons, you walk
into the room.

Part Three

Aquatic Park: 1967

This is the dead poet's academy
at five o'clock. Here comes the fog. Two winos
and a curly long-haired kid
have scrap fires going on the sand. A fat
Italian sitting on the *Chronicle*
on the sparse grass turns up
his transistor radio to hear
the baseball scores. I
never met him. He named
you, you brought me here; his ghost
is what we leave on the littered slope, watching
the digestion of the bay, watching
the drunk poets come back. Bringing
brandy.

                                   Seagulls
                                   circle
                                   Long
                                   Pier.

One nurses the
brandy while his boy
friend does cartwheels. They
want to be taken to dinner. We
can't afford it. They
try being ebullient. We
really can't afford it. They
stay in the graying park, one

squatting on the grass with the bottle
between his knees, the other
standing on his hands. We
go off rail-balancing, leaving
the brandy, into our
biographical information.

Iceplants: Army Beach

Your body glistens like a new
subway token, nipples the color of copper
turned out of the light. You
ring true skimming the sea, splashing
and pulling me after. Your
wet shoulders incite me to spurious literature
while jeweled ice spatters my belly and thighs.
The black thatch
at your crotch sparkles;
your cock shrivels. We are standing still. We dare
each other in, stung numb
by sea-foam.
Like jumping off a wall I wouldn't
try I ran
into the cold sea up to my eyes and fell
off a sand-bar. Behind me
you grabbed my hand and pulled
me to my feet, drawing
me back in that clasp
to the shore.
Our hands are the same size.

To say
I fell asleep on the beach
and woke
to see your narrow hips blocking the sky:

a lie. Past driftwood,
at the cracks the tide slapped on the shore,
you stood against a flag of sand and sky,
etched dark on the sea.

Behind the cliffs iceplants clutch the dunes
to shape. We face embankments of cement
with dynamited doors. From catacombs
under fake hills, an army watched the sea.
We stagger through a passage in the dark,
around a corner, toward a gap of light,
a two-foot hole. We crouch and clamber out.
Here were gun emplacements. On the walls
around the rift, chalked, SURFERS SUCK DICK
JOHNNY AND MICKI. And the shifting hills
held with rooted tongues of red and green.
Below, the city falls away
white on slopes under the seamist.
There is a poem in touching
or not touching. The poem
defines the tension between skin and skin,
increasing, decreasing, rhythmically
changing the space it defines.
This puts us on the edge of the cliff
crunching iceplants underfoot. Between
camouflaged gun-turrets, two boys cruise
each other. How much of the poem
is about touching or not
touching? Fifty feet below
in the glint of waves through mist, a naked man
with a wristwatch and a walking-stick
approaches, but will not reach,
two horses spurred through the foam.

The Art of the Novel
for Bill Brodecky

The afternoon breaks from a pale
morning on the water of maps
hanging above the desk. Cities
interest him more than people. Geography
is a kind of vast gossip. I always
gossip in poems, mostly about myself, //
hinting at inadmissible longings.
I want Everything. Every day
this week I woke up so happy
I felt guilty; warm legs
wrapped around mine. I can't
stay in this beautiful city forever.

I am inventing a city
in these lines. The people
are half real, living
in my correspondent city, created
for them with streets and buildings,
trees and the necessary harbor.
They frequent a bar and perhaps a beach, but I
take them from one place to the other.
You can draw an accurate map and say:
This is where *she* lives with her young German
from Buenos Aires. Five blocks away
in a converted carriage house with a back garden

lives an older painter who covets them both,
usually confusing love and politics.

It is almost always a spring morning. Will I ever
start to work early? We remember the pale
profile out of Goethe. He can't
make his head a compass, disparages maps
and gets seasick on Green St. I have land legs
now, imagining a network of double cities
from here to Leningrad. I might be happy
writing novels, if I could color into geography
like the plate of fruit I painted yesterday.
It is almost always
a spring morning, in the air a longing
to confuse myself.

Before the War

We are asleep under mirrors. What do I
look like? Your mouth
opens on a dream of altered landscapes.
Hidden in the Iron Mountains,
the adolescent general is in love
with you. Noon light stands in the window,
cloudy and white. They are using mustard gas.
That night child anarchists besieged the corners.
Tin cans exploded in front of us; rhythm
escaped in the blistered rain. Everyone
was hungry. You sound
like that in the morning, someone
told her on the telephone, and all
the bar heard it Friday night.
Culled from a garden in Pacific Heights,
the charred corpse of her last lover, ankles crossed
at a vulnerable and tender angle,
embellishes the service porch
above an architecture of dead boys.
It happens every morning at the gas
station while we are still asleep
around the pillow like a third lover.
Covered in burning Saran Wrap,
the young attendant knocks the telephone
off the hook, crashes through
the plate-glass window

and flames out like a screaming Bunsen burner
under the open hood of a '39
Renault sedan. I wake up with your elbow
under my neck. Come here.
Tell me what that eruption on the sun
is.

Landscape for Insurrection

While they drank themselves into a fog,
we planned: Could we survive in the hills?
They stood in the embrasure of the bay
window. I thought of the long climb.
Those uniforms! black brocade on a red ground
and leather hipboots scored with stars.

This is a transformation. Daystars
are crumbling on the rocks above the fog
as damp hands score my shoulders to the ground.
I am out of breath. In a valley between hills
there is a walled town. Mornings we will climb
the rocks to count tankers entering the bay;

I'll seed a plot with spices, dill and bay
and chervil. Now the slopes are spiced with stars.
Light corners the next rise that we climb.
Prickly grasses part, releasing fog
that wreaths around the leveling of the hills
and humps up the slopes close to the ground.

Winded again, I only ground
my teeth and kept going. Dogs began to bay
from the valley at the disappearing hills.
The swollen moon and punctured stars

dangle above the hilltops and the fog
that swallows our long shadows as we climb

and spits them back into the valley. "Climb
up here a minute! What are these tracks on the ground?"
Instead, we sit on a rock, watching fog
track up from the ocean highway and the bay.
"I used to know the names of all the stars."
"Funny, nobody ever named these hills."

In a wrecked lean-to on the highest hill
we hide our things, and smoke outside. Lights climb
up from the bridge, planes pass between the stars.
We rake a pile of stuff left on the ground:
shoe, cartridge, paper, keeping bugs at bay
with cigarette smoke curling into fog.

Covered by fog, we will come down from the hills
into the dark towns on the bay. To find us, you must climb
to this cleared high ground, marked with flares like stars.

The Sea Coming Indoors

The war is far away, sweet
birdsong around the villas on the cliff.
Breakers crash below the dining room
where a gawky Filipino girl
rearranges and rearranges
silver forks on a white linen cloth.
I have given her
your skin, but your mouth
curves around a secret. Speak.
Tapping the salad forks
on her thin left wrist, she paces
the length of the window; a yard away
the drop behind glass
turns her stomach, and a vision
recurs: she is climbing down
the cliff in a gold dress, loose rocks
and thorn bushes bite her palms, these new
shoes will slip, little slides
of dirt and pebbles brush her ankles.
                                        You
will not come back, decked
with garnets and thorn bushes, hefting
a live grenade. When
you take off your shirt, I see
a line of tiny rubies set
in the central furrow of your chest.

See, my hands are empty. I close
my eyes and forget what I am holding
You are not here. Gem grains
crease my palm. I am looking at you.
Salt air wreaths the door as it opens.
A gap flickers in skin. Elegant
insects twitch to life
in rock shells on the slope. She huddles
on a ledge, unfolding
like a kite before herself unfolding
her hands. It is too late. The seeds
of her disease cling to her wet palms
at the edges of vision. I am sitting
in front of the window, counting
silverware. I have given her
your skin.

Attack on the Iron Coast

The trees are waiting. Three
brown horses, ridden by
twelve-year-old girls with long
brown hair, shoulder each other
at the tide's edge. This
ocean was always
heartbreaking. The rocks
are waiting. Wedged
in a sandy shelf halfway
up the cliff, full of buried
shells and sand-dollars, two people
are waiting. The sun
is an incandescent
solid. On top of the cliff,
in front of the billowed
barbed wire, banging the backs
of their bare calves on the rock-face,
four people are
waiting. The tar road
west of the lake, leading
between the hidden bunkers to the dwarf
pine grove, is empty. A motorcycle
lies on its side on crushed
iceplants next to the road. Inside
the buried passage to the fort, broken
cinder blocks and fused

sandbags frame the still
city beyond the trees east of the lake,
glowing blue and gold. Blue-white
with darkening maroon strokes, naked
to the waist, a man sprawls
on the broken rocks. His skin
is blue-white, the knife slashes
maroon. Flies hover in the clean air, waiting.

Pornographic Poem

You are walking
down the corridor. A man
in striped boxer shorts comes
out closing the last door. It is
the bathroom. Not really
the last door; the corridor
turns there. Your room
is beyond the turn. The third
door on the left. A blond
boy with long hair in faded
jeans and no shirt walks out of the
bathroom, turns. The man
passes you as the boy turns; he
has a crew cut. You are sweating,
your feet are damp in old sandals.
There are no windows in the corridor;
it is underground. Below it
is another corridor, and below
that. Above it
is another corridor. You think
of the window in your room. You can
have a window because of the
hill. At night, if you are
alone, you explore
levels you have not yet seen, under
the DC bulbs. Sometimes

you pass a person on the dark stairs, but
usually not. Barefoot
on the faded figured rug, you can
stop in front of a closed door, hear
a saucepan clank on a hotplate, skin
sliding in sheets, somebody
swallowing, coughing. You always
save the last level for next time. Old men
stay on the upper
levels. A tanned
young man with curly black hair
goes into the bathroom. You
slow down. You go into
the bathroom.

Forage Sestina

This is for your body hidden in words
moving through a crumbling structure.
Between heaps of plaster, chicken-wire
snaggles the gaping floor. Stripped of beams,
cement encloses more cement. A wall
mounds up between parlor and dining-room.

Explicit shadows grapple through the room
which is a ruined city. Falling words
erode veined gullies in the nearer wall.
This is to see if only structure
communicates. Under a beam
an outlet spouts tongues of stripped wire

and your breath crackles like a shorted wire.
You are standing behind me, even in this room
which is a camouflage. Signal beams
flash through the casement, and our words
cadence them, shushed with light, making a structure
of light and sound bouncing off the bare wall.

I want to touch you, but you are the wall
crumbling, the report over the wire
service that there were no survivors. Structure
demands that we remain inside the room,

that you cannot be hedged in easy words
like skin or hands, that we cannot look through the beams

of the burnt roof and see stars. All the beams
were hauled off. Concrete floor, ceiling, walls
surround us. There is one window. Words
cannot be trusted. Capillaries wire
swiveling eyes. If we search this room
we may be able to plot out the structure

of the whole building. We were told that the structure
is flawed, that the searchlight beam
from the bridge pierces cracks. If the room
begins to rotate, floor becoming wall
et cetera, and white sparks dribble from torn wires,
there has been a rebellion of words.

Words will peel off you, revealing the structure
of a human body branched with wires. Over the last beam
keeping the sky from the walls, vines drip into the room.

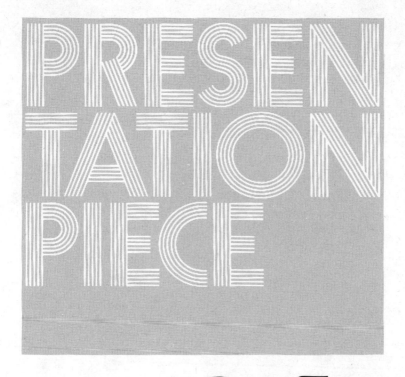

Part Four

Imaginary Translation I

for Gerald L. Fabian

These foothills shelter me from war and love.
The pig-boy doesn't trouble my sleep, nor does
his sister, slinging pears in a wicker basket.
That orchard rolls below my garden
where I spent this morning pruning
the rose-of-Sharon bushes I transplanted
from the pasture above Agate Cove.
Once a week the post comes from the city:
Joseph, my redhead cousin with the nose,
has joined the Army. Lifkin's second book
was mentioned twice at Madame G's soirée.
And R has made acquaintance with an actress.
(Dear R, it is less painful now to think of
your eyes, and your abominable French.)
This afternoon I walked up in the hills
along the coast. Gorse-bush and choke-robin
and robber's-purse were all in bloom.
I caught a tan lizard and let him go
and watched three butter-colored butterflies
converge over a whitened dog-turd.
Along the skin-hued strip of beach below,
a scraggly green platoon down from the fort
was firing ragged rounds into the tide.

Imaginary Translation II

Those men and boys who are
your week-end lovers, I wish
them affluence and patience
to charm you and to learn from you
and teach
you by reflection how you move;
and that woman who turns
open-eyed in your arms in your green room
as pine boughs crackle at the city fog,
I wish
her a long sojourn in a summer country
with someone faithful, blond and tall,
gentle and exigent
and not you.

Imaginary Translation III
for Bill Brodecky and for Tom Disch

There was no reason to stay in that city
any longer. I had concluded my affairs
well enough. I knew no one but colleagues,
and the foggy season
was starting. That last night, fortified with brandy,
I took a late walk on the waterfront.
Boats lowed; the triple-masted shadows
of long-beached ironclads striped the streets.
Next to a bar I'd heard of was the theater.
You know the plot, how the traveler,
too rich or too poor, goes to a foreign theater
and, from front row center, or the rear balcony,
sees that the star, or the last one in the chorus,
is that person, touched and held perhaps three days,
but loved (the traveler knows now) all these years.
It was not three days, but three years
we were lovers, and barely one apart,
with a few thousand intervening miles.
But there was the name on a list of names.
And the ticket window was open. I went in.
The loge was obviously best. Much leather
and brocade; faces I would not
recognize under elaborate hair,
feathers and smoke and lace. Many seats
were empty. I could imagine, seated
in the dusty maroon cut-velvet

armchair—you know the story. Then
they milled onstage, shrilling a language
not the one the audience was chattering
and neither of them mine. Footlights swallowed
sweet hashish and contraband tobacco:
a whiteflossed creature, breasts like apricots,
pelted as St. Sebastian. When the arrows
whistled—those gold wounds were not real,
but they bled. *Shoot first who loves me best.*
The archer had green-scaled metallic breasts,
green shoes, green flower headdress, a blond beard
and silver eyes. I did not think, "What monster
have you become?"—only tried to find
those brown arms and attenuated thighs
in the rush of particoloured limbs.
"There," as somebody in fuchsia satin
tossed back black hair; but was it you or I
who pushed their hair out of their eyes like that?
And those were certainly the wrong ankles
on the blackfaced dancer. The laugh
was right. And the singing voice,
if you had ever learned to sing. You would
have had those eyes, if you had blue eyes.
Perhaps it was three days and not three years
I knew you, and your language was my second
language; perhaps your lover lived
in another city, and your copper
hair covered your forehead as we danced.
But we grew up in the country with the same
foster-parents, always suspecting
our mother was the same, until we first
laid damp palms on each other.
The footlights dimmed; some of them clumped
to sing, while spotlit dancers cruised the aisles

accosting those whose income or whose gender
was too plain. I was safe in the loge
from scented satin thrown over my face
pushed into pungent ambiguities
in which I tasted you. The story ends
with the pilgrim discovered and embraced
by the stellar lover, with the voyager
carrying off the aging *rat de ballet*
or sneaking away unrecognized: "Who *is*
that person? Surely someone I know?"
I walked out through the incense and liqueurs
with everyone who did not stay. The fuchsia
satin (whose hair was kinkier than yours),
the blackface, the albino Cupidon,
the naked skull, the rouged and bearded diva
lounged to coffee and brandy at a bar.
I looked at them. They looked at me. I walked
out, towards home, in the sequined fog
of this city, which is, by now, mine.

To the Reader

Pacing from room to room trimming the plants,
I walk heavily on my heels. I smoke
foul-smelling French cigarettes. Invoke
that portly bluestocking in gardening pants.
Won't do. And if Catullus learns to cook
while Lesbia goes to the bars to cruise,
you haven't put up anything to lose
except two hours to read a different book.
Boys will be boys and wonder in their rooms
if fame could be a sociable disease.
"I'll sleep alone and murder whom I please
and find another lover when the moon's
in Scorpio." Be grateful to our Mom.
She let you off with cancer and the bomb.

Nightsong

A plant will draw back vision to its source
and crack the glass if it is very tall
to grow by moonlight whose sufficient force
prevents my eyes from banging on the wall.
There is an undulant red satin back
that, exoskeletally ribbed in gold,
incites the digits' giggling maniac
to hold to have to hold to have to hold
to have cold water thicken on his tongue
until his anal gravy binds the sky
while no one looks particularly young
and certainly not you, friend bone, nor I.
Although you sweat and pant and show your skull
and tease your hair with overheated birds,
it's not my fault that you are beautiful
as a refrigerator full of words.
I was a polyglotted acrobat
who hoofed on a technicians' tour of hell,
but now I'm going to drop the alphabet
and stay at home and teach my wound to spell.
And if you think my singing voice is nice
and want to comb my hair and think I'm sane,
I'll cool my ears by sucking on some ice
and let you borrow someone else's brain.

The Muses

C'est Vénus toute entière à sa proie attachée . . .
—RACINE, *Phèdre*

Don't think I haven't noticed you
waiting in the other room to kill me.
She came too close to the root, my sister,
rooting in the coals for a pristine
death, wishing, oh, wishing
it wasn't so flabby,
the skin creases gone livid and all
those sensual surfaces puckering
like a plucked chicken
(and that was what she
  thought of seeing a
  limp cock for the
  first time: a
  turkey neck).
Now I stand in front of the
oven, warming
my hands. At my desk
after sundown, my nails turn blue.
And you are waiting in
one of the other
rooms. Sometimes you are a
middle-aged woman, your skin
flabby, bluish, your hair
frizzed out in filaments, picking up
whispers of plots to Do You In
you can almost hear. You pat your face

feeling the puckers and creases, knowing
it is already Too Late, even
if it is only Tuesday, when you dreamed
it was Friday.
                    Sometimes
you are a Beautiful Boy, out of a
pederast's fantasy, dark-curled
golden and edible, mouth
curved in a snarl or a lie. Rage
wrinkles your cheeks in a newborn's imperative howl
and to placate you, I can only say Yes
I will curl my hair, lend you twenty dollars, Yes
the world is ending, fashion is all, if
I were honest I would starve myself to death.

And one of you
will tear out chunks of my hair, and one
of you will slap me across the eyes, and
one of you will hit my head with a rock
at the top of the stairs and
one of you will kick me in the stomach
and one of you will smash at my nails
with a lead paperweight. O lying
at the foot of the stairs, my legs
wedged against the door, fingers
sticky against my eyelids, listening
to you tear up the rest of the house, I
will not be convinced
by your onyx
identical eyes.

Later

Later,
while it is still
morning I fill the chunky glass
pitcher and water
the plants. The purple coleus
on my desk gets too much
sun, though the green and white
ones thrive. I move
over thresholds. Each room is alive
in a different
season. The dieffenbachia
is pushing a new
leaf at last. Above
where you sat, the chrysanthemum,
teased to baroque
arabesques by northeast light,
grapples the glass. Last
I turn the kitchen succulents,
then feed the cats. I snip
some of the gray one's brow hair
for Helen from New Orleans downstairs to make
a potion. Lolling
alert in her purple chair, she
tells me, don't use it before Sunday and
especially don't taste it; or I will
hurl myself at the window, my heart
hammering like this morning, growling Kill.

Waiting

I get up every day before the mail
and go through the same matinal ritual:
piss, wash, make coffee, warm my hands,
prune and water my three rooms of plants,
feed the cats, answer yesterday's letters.
Something frightening is going to happen.

But nothing extraordinary will happen
today. There's no interesting mail:
a postcard, bills, very professional letters
that only want a kind of ritual
reply. I chew my pen and watch the plants
and would like very much to put my hands

in dirt or in someone else's hands.
I don't know what it is I want to happen.
I think that I am safe behind the plants.
There was no coded message in the mail
today. "You have let your part of the ritual
lapse. We are informed by certain letters

the key to the kabbalistic letters
has fallen into uninitiate hands.
Purify yourself with the first ritual
cleansing. We may not say what will happen
and cannot contact you except by mail.
Beware of interceptions and of plants."

I wish I lived alone with growing plants.
I wish I had a lover instead of letters
from strangers. The arrival of the mail
is the only time that someone hands
me movement. Nothing real is going to happen
yet, except this desiccated ritual.

Later, I preserve my wit in ritual
dissection. The cats sleep in the plants.
The fog burns off toward evening. If I happen
to say: impatience and despair, in letters
to strangers, I am putting myself in their hands.
Dismissals and evictions come by mail.

Mail this now. Then I will tell you the ritual.
Rub your hands with leaves from these three plants.
Wait for their letters. Tell me what happens.

Like Aschenbach in Arizona

My two companions are tireless, and the landscape
makes the human form irrelevant
except as a naked surreal intrusion.
Still, I remember you. Yesterday,
we walked through the Petrified Forest.
Between foothills of striated clay,
logs turn to semi-precious stone;
molecule by molecule, crystal
pervades the wood. After an hour, our bodies
were covered with fine white alkaloid dust.
The sky was bluer than your eyes. The process
continues. Cerebral crenellations
crunched under our feet. I could imagine
parts of your body grown massive,
translucent, severed, defined. Bloodstone
searing the veins. "I'm not your bloody Muse,"
you said, and indeed you aren't.
"But I will be." Well, here you are,
a jet trail above the highway,
preceding us to California.
I'll never see you again. When I came back
from scrabbling toward the sky up a bleached mound,
Tom was examining a quartz block
blotched with agate and amethyst. "If the light
never changed, I'd go mad in an hour."
We talked about drugs and poetry. The sky

is bluer than your eyes. I am using you. The process
continues. The hills heaved in the sun.
It is harder than the stoned mind imagines
to sink into a landscape. The dust will not
accept you. The stones will not accept you.
There is not enough time between breaths
to feel the crystalloid osmosis
begin. My heartbeat calls me back,
the pounding in my ears, the sweat
sliding down my ribs. And here I am,
a small, redheaded, pungent woman, not
your bloody Muse. Today
the three of us climbed down into the Grand Canyon
about a mile, after our hangovers.
The sun seeped into me like orange juice.
Swifts sliced the clean air.
I interpose a figure, charged
with repercussive energy, imposing
human-scale on a landscape.
Charles posed Tom and me on the lip of the gorge
for tourist shots. This piece of petrified wood
in my hand is hot and smooth
rust-mottled milk with crinkled apertures
I stick my fingers in. Tonight, we'll be in Las Vegas.

PRESENTATION PIECE

Part Five

Sestina

for D.G.B.

For a week now our bodies have whispered
together, telling each other secrets
you and I would keep. Their language,
harder and more tender than this, wakes
us suddenly in the half-dawn, tangled
dragons on their map. They have a plan.

We are stranded travelers who plan
to ditch our bags and walk. The hill wind whispers
danger and rain. We are going different ways. That
       tangled
thornbush is where the road forks. The secrets
we told on the station bench to keep awake
were lies. I suspect from your choice of language

that you are not speaking your native language.
You will not know about the city plan
tattooed behind my knee. But the skin wakes
up in humming networks, audibly whispers
over the dead wind. Everybody's secrets
jam the wires. Syllables get tangled

with bus tickets and matchbooks. You tangled
my hair in your fingers and language
split like a black fig. I suck the secrets
off your skin. This isn't in the plan,

the subcutaneous transmitter whispers.
Be circumspect. What sort of person wakes

up twice in a wrecked car? And we wake
in wary seconds of each other, tangled
damply together. Your cock whispers
inside my thigh that there is language
without memory. Your fingers plan
wet symphonies in my garrulous secret

places. There is nothing secret
in people crying at weddings and singing at wakes;
and when you pack a duffelbag and plan
on the gratuitous, you will still tangle
purpose and habit, more baggage, more language.
It is not accidental what they whisper.

Our bodies whispered under the sheet. Their secret
language will not elude us when we wake
into the tangled light without a plan.

Villanelle
for D.G.B.

Every day our bodies separate,
exploded torn and dazed.
Not understanding what we celebrate

we grope through languages and hesitate
and touch each other, speechless and amazed;
and every day our bodies separate

us farther from our planned, deliberate
ironic lives. I am afraid, disphased,
not understanding what we celebrate

when our fused limbs and lips communicate
the unlettered power we have raised.
Every day our bodies' separate

routines are harder to perpetuate.
In wordless darkness we learn wordless praise,
not understanding what we celebrate;

wake to ourselves, exhausted, in the late
morning as the wind tears off the haze,
not understanding how we celebrate
our bodies. Every day we separate.

Sisterhood

for Dora FitzGerald

No place for a lady, this
back-country gateway comes
up from dreams; the wounds
are an entrance, or a season ticket.
The morning freshness, the
summersend mountain calm:
distractions. "What do you
call this town?"

No man will love you, no
woman be your friend, your
face will go away, your body
betray you. We wrestled
to the floor, his fingers
blanching my elbows, cords
popping his neck. Don't look
into the sun. Don't squint.

He lay on the concrete
ramp of the bus terminal. I
massaged his back and shoulders through his clothes.
I opened his trenchcoat, peeled
its collar away from his thin
white shirt, his thin chest.
Staining the slashed white
yellowish pink, those wounds.

When you give the ghost
bread and water he asks
for, you incur prophecy.
"Why have you come here,
woman? Your city
is far away. We do not speak
your language. Your sister
is dead.

"Take off your rings
at the first gate. At the second,
your crown of lapis lazuli.
You must leave your golden
breastplate at the third, and below
the gallows where he hangs
who forgot you, and will not rise,
break your mother's scepter."

They have killed him
often. He bled
on the concrete floor. My hands
were not healing. They took him
into the next room. I heard
gunshots. I woke screaming.
At the bottom of hell
he swings in the stinking wind. She watches.

We, women, never
trust his returnings. He takes
the bread and water, but
the words on the paper
are illegible. His body
lies severed on the white sand

and the pieces are not
food, they are stones.

We gather those
jewels and wear them,
lapis in the crown, amethysts
over the nipples, garnets
oozing on cool
fingers. The gateway
dreams itself up, and we eye the surly
guard, and strip, and go down.

Elegy

for Janis Joplin

Crying from exile, I
mourn you, dead singer, crooning and palming
your cold cheeks, calling you: You.
A man told me you died; he was
foreign, I felt for the first time, drunk, in his car, my
throat choked: You won't sing for me
now. Later I laughed in the hair between
his shoulder-blades, well enough
loved in a narrow
bed; it was
your Southern Comfort
grin stretching my
mouth. You were in me
all night,

shouting our pain, sucking off
the mike, telling a strong-headed
woman's daily beads to dumb kids
creaming on your high
notes. Some morning at wolf-hour
they'll know.
Stay in my
gut, woman lover I never
touched, tongued, or sang to; stay
in back of my
throat, sandpaper

velvet, Janis, you
overpaid your
dues, damn it, why are you dead?

Cough up your whisky gut
demon, send him home howling
to Texas, to every
fat bristle-chinned
white motel keeper on
Route 66, every half-
Seminole waitress with a
crane's neck, lantern-jawed
truck driver missing a
finger joint, dirt-farmer's
blond boy with asthma and sea dreams,
twenty-one-year-old
mother of three who got far
as Albuquerque once.

Your veins were
highways from
Coca-Cola flatland,
dust and dead
flies crusting the
car window till it rained.
Drive! anywhere
out of here, the
ratty upholstery smelling
of dogpiss and cunt,
bald tires swiveled and
lurched on slicked macadam
skidding the funk in your mouth
to a black woman's tongue.

Faggots and groupies and
meth heads loved you, you
loved bodies and booze
and hard work, and more
than that, fame. On your
left tit was a tattooed
valentine, around your
wrist a tattooed filigree; around
your honeycomb brain webbed
klieg lights and amp circuits screamed
Love Love and the booze-
skag-and-cocaine baby twisted your
box, kicked your
throat and the songs came.

I wanted to write your
blues, Janis, and put my
tongue in your mouth that way.
Lazy and grasping and
treacherous, beautiful
insomniac freaking the ceiling,
the cold smog went slowly blue, the cars
caught up with your heartbeat, maybe you were not
alone, but the ceiling told you
otherwise, and skag said:
You are more famous than anyone
out of West Texas, your hair is a
monument, your voice preserved
in honey, I love you, lie down.

I am in London and
you, more meat than Hollywood
swallowed, in Hollywood, more
meat. You got me through

long nights with your coalscuttle
panic, don't be scared
to scream when it hurts
and oh mother it hurts, tonight
we are twenty-seven, we are
alone, you are dead.

Nimue to Merlin

Who are you anyway? Did it take long
to get here? I don't live in a tower,
but I don't have Thursday salons either.
I take care of my plants. I'm not as young
as I look, and I like to be alone
most of the time. May I fix you a drink?

Shoo off the cat. I usually don't drink
before dinner, but I've had a long
day, working. Are you traveling alone?
I've heard about you. Once, I saw your tower
from the high road, when I was very young
and curious. I'm glad that I'm not either

now. And here you are, which means you've either
changed, or you want something. I wouldn't drink
so fast if I were you. How young
you look. Your skin is like a boy's, and long
hair becomes you. If you stood up, you would tower
over me. Don't you find, when you're alone

long, you lose eyes and voices, let alone
people's tastes and smells. Excuse me, I'll either
embarrass myself or you. In your tower
when it's almost dawn, and you can't drink

or sleep more (I'm presuming) and it's a long
way down, and some idiotic young

bird shrills up, do you think, when you were young,
if you'd let it hurt, let well enough alone,
things would have gotten better before long?
You wouldn't be here now. I don't think so either.
Here's pears and cheese. I'll make another drink.
Your hands are cold. Your neck is stiff as a tower.

It's already late. The road back to the tower
is crowded with political loud young
men with no wives who've had too much to drink.
Do you want to go back there tonight alone?
I won't keep you. I won't chase you, either.
Sometimes the nights here are extremely long.

Lie alongside me. I'll build you a tower
in my hand. You're either too old or too young
to be alone here. Open your mouth. Let me drink.

Rooms in Bloomsbury

The horrors of the personal, revealed
in indiscreetly published *cahiers*,
lean on the pristine chronicle. "Today
A and Z used my room instead. I feel
nothing, although I saw them on the bed
one instant before switching off the light
again. Read Stendhal in the bath all night."
As, circumspectly in that epoch, Z
writes, ". . . then, at last, they published it, and for
the first time public notice shaped my life,
till world events intruded. Even C
could not ignore the change, and, as for me,
I soon displeased my publishers, my wife
and friends, enlisted and endured the War."

Aube Provençale

Absent, this morning
the cock crowed later than the nine o'clock
church bells. Cherry boughs
bronzed outside the casement,
and I woke

sweating, with my hands
between my thighs, from a dream
of archives, wanting you
under me, my breasts hollowed in the arc
below your ribs,

my knees between your knees,
my hands behind your ears, my cheek
furrowed in your chest, tasting
our mingled night-sweat, tasting
your sleep.

I'll make a song
on your neck-cords. Wake up,
bird asleep against my hip-bone,
and crow, it's already
morning.

Crépuscule Provençale

Cursing the Mistral,
the neighbor elbows doorward.
It batters on tiled roofs, whips cascades
across the hill-face. Meet me
near the sea,

I wrote; come to me
through polyglot gossip,
and we'll share mountains, oceans, islands.
November is wind and rain
here. Heavy

persimmons, bloody
on black branches, gleamed in blue
afternoon, clear as a hidden valley.
Lapis beyond the green gorge, the sea spilled
its chalice

of hills. It's a month
since I left you, near water, wet
pebbles in our pockets, I'll write, our cheeks
brushed, salt gusts already
between us.

Dark now, shutters bang
stucco. Later I'll drink

by the fire, and let three tongues of
chatter silence an absence sung
in the wind.

Apologia pro opere suo

It appears that almost all the poets who slighted
the theme of Unrequited Love to say
how more of the land than That Boy or That Lady lay
were poets whom somebody had, in fact, requited.
The eclogue on The Natural Order of Things
and The Imperfectibility of Man
ends with blond wife and prepubescent son
waiting with soup and a snifter in the wings.
While William had his visions, Kate baked bread.
Chester is clever with scores and escargots.
Mary kept the books, and wrote one, too.
From the querulous to the universal "You"
is not an unthinkably long distance to go
when the Muse gets up first and brings you breakfast
        in bed.

The Osiris Complex

No coastline ever
lost a man like this
desert; the sea makes
definitions. Sky
wrapped his neck, sand
tunneled up his bare
chest, slanting against the wind. Were there
bones, were there rocks
that looked like bones, did
limbs shimmer, severed
at sight's periphery?
His body seemed irrelevant, pain
was not real, nor remembered
palms, his nipples hardening
into the life-line. Sky and white
distances of sand, the wind
mixing them, the line
between them going on
perhaps forever, some interstellar
measurement. "Infinity is the
bogeyman of the precocious
child," she said later.
And he: "Naked
in the hot wind, a wooden
staff in my hand, language
retreated in my forehead,

a milky stone, a blind eye."
Were there birds, were there
watery sand-blooms, were there
polished stones the color of blood and eyes?
Only the ancient
weight, the absence
of metaphor, a visible
reddening behind the lids, the wind
changing everything. The wind did not change anything.
(She came with the
rec squad, in the
first jeep, broad little
burnt face, like those
Cambodian girl commandos, axle grease
up to the elbows.
"Pick up those rocks, pick up
all those damned rocks, get them
into the truck." And to herself, "Why
have you brought me here? Last
at the edge of a cliff, those rocks with the ocean
foaming below in impossible
colors. Why
have you brought me here? This catalogue:
one obsidian
femur, a truncated
jasper calf, onyx
haunch powdered with dried blood. Build
a city, let it cover
the earth, make islands.
Obliterate this landscape.")
Were there, finally,
words, arrowy black
motes on the sky? Even the smooth
stones only rattled in his head, he willed

his limbs away, they didn't
go. A corpse keeps
its scars. Riddled with diamond
grains, wind-striped, stripped, sun-forgotten,
lassitude
weighed on his
pivots; he was
screened from his own
pain, by his own pain.
Heavier, heavier, his
ankles belonged to the sand, his calves took root,
his thighs were hollowed by the wind. Bright
pebbles rattled in the bone cage, sang
him to the rock. Yes, with words.
(She came back, alone, at
nightfall. The soldiers
were asleep, dreaming dark girls
licking salt from their elbows.
She came back, black
as lava, twice as old,
tall, tall and
haggard, too
black to look at, hooded
in her own face. "In these
sockets his eyes
elude me. I cannot
describe how the stones
in my hands become dead
meat, keening to be
born. I am an old, bald
horror, as human as
he was, still hungry.
Why have you brought me here?")
"Why have you brought me here?"

he did not say, questioning
his naked arms, juxtaposed
on all that sand, shifting its
topography, all that flat
dazzling
sky. He knew if he
lay down, something
might, or might not
happen.
He would spin centrifugally
into those pricks of
white light, shaken from the
surface, another
sand-whirl. He would
sweep into those distances.
How dense it was, a place in back of the head
where it all goes on; unnecessary warmth,
too heavy, too bright, eyes
balk at it. It was closed, it would not
let go. He finally
let go, finally
put the khaki shirt and shorts back on,
walked barefoot back to camp through the
cooling sand, holding his shoes.
(She did not
come at all. The rocks cast
ambiguous shadows in the
mellowing light,
uninterrupted. Thousands of miles away,
a ten-year-old, chewing the bedclothes, staring
at the projections of infinite
space on the ceiling, asked
the stranger in the cave behind her
eyes, "Why have you brought me here?")

Untoward Occurrence
at Embassy Poetry Reading

Thank you. Thank you very much. I'm pleased
to be here tonight. I seldom read
to such a varied audience. My poetry
is what it is. Graves, yes, said love, death
and the changing of the seasons
were the unique, the primordial subjects.

I'd like to talk about that. One subjects
oneself to art, not necessarily pleased
to be a colander for myths. It seasons
one to certain subjects. Not all. You can read
or formulate philosophies; your death
is still the kernel of your dawn sweats. Poetry

is interesting to people who write poetry.
Others are involved with other subjects.
Does the Ambassador consider death
on the same scale as you, Corporal? Please
stay seated. I've outreached myself. I read
your discomfort. But tonight the seasons

change. I've watched you, in town for the season,
nod to each other, nod to poetry
represented by me, and my colleagues, who read
to good assemblies; good citizens, good subjects

for gossip. You're the audience. Am I pleased
to frighten you? Yes and no. It scares me to death

to stand up here and talk about real death
while our green guerrillas hurry up the seasons.
They have disarmed the guards by now, I'm pleased
to say. The doors are locked. Great poetry
is not so histrionic, but our subjects
choose us, not otherwise. I will not read

manifestos. Tomorrow, foreigners will read
rumors in newspapers. . . . Oh, sir, your death
would be a tiresome journalistic subject,
so stay still till we're done. This is our season.
The building is surrounded. No more poetry
tonight. We are discussing, you'll be pleased

to know, the terms of your release. Please read
these leaflets. Not poetry. You're bored to death
with politics, but that's the season's subject.

A Christmas Crown

I

Son of the dark solstice descends the tree
into the winter city. Riversedge
receives him as the rusty currents dredge
our frozen offal heavily to sea.
Child of our Mother in the death of light,
torn out of blood onto a shattered mirror,
squall reasonable hungers to our terror;
it will not take so long tomorrow night.
The starry dragon will be drawn to scale,
exhaling central heating on the crib
or carton where the infant graingod breathes
and coughs up stringy gobbets on the wreaths,
decides to live; earth-warmed air swells his ribs
while she smiles at the moon, her plate, her pale.

II

While she smiles at the moon, her plate, her pale
reflection, tideridden ladylove
of corner boys and epileptics, of
remittance princes, alcoholics, frail
dexedrine beauties, we in lust of male
muses had best rededicate
postponed mornings. This time she might not wait.
In her thin arms the child begins to wail,
robust and greedy, sucking every sin
but hope out of her teeming hemisphere.
Will he rebuild our city where we stand
ritually dumfounded by the hand-
reflexes of any infant? Where
will he learn our hunger, and begin?

III

Will he learn our hunger and begin
the politic ascent? Our history
glyphs our bodies; querent to him we
flash autonomic broadcasts. On the skin
of a distracted shopgirl: Monday's news,
produce of Sussex, a sermon on Greed.
I praise you, baby who still cannot read,
accept, acclaim, admonish, or accuse.
I have my woman's winter in my hands;
my mouth bleeds with a homeless appetite;
the several importunities of lust
grease my regard. In solitary trust,
I pledge infidel vigil as the night,
swollen with day-birth, chills, cajoles, commands.

IV
Swollen with day, birth chills, cajoles, commands
simpler directions. We still want to go
back to the Good Place. We could finish grow-
ing up in an orderly, four-seasoned land-
scape, we tell each other, drinking gin-
and-limes on the terrace while the monster flock
moves through the hot rain to the western dock.
Here we are languid adolescents in
fiction, waiting for a Protagonist
to get us moving. Outside, the real snow
drifts to the real street. They've closed the bars,
and whisky voices slide above the cars'
tarry andante, caroling her slow
pains as she brings her belly to the tryst.

V

Pain. As she brings her belly to the tryst,
invalids, children, and insomniacs
turn in their beds, wanting the daylight back;
and lovers, whose replenishment consists
of little sleeps between betraying dreams,
wake, thinking that blue window is another
blue window, and that heavy kiss is Mother's
send-off on a class hike in the Extremes.
More would be only fiction: how the dying,
the pious, the powerful, turn on their own
wheels of year-dark, emerge, or stay behind.
I don't know what the nursling in my mind
will grow to, only question an unknown
quality, voiced with a newborn's crying.

VI

Quality voiced with a newborn's crying,
impotent as an infant to reply
to questions or the chocolate-covered lie:
O wouldn't it be cozy to stop trying,
O give the music-sheets, the cup, the child
back to the nice lady and come *on*
(who on the wet steps to the Underground
in Baker Street turned with jonquils and smiled).
When I have grown accustomed to the cold,
when I have grown accustomed to the dark,
the lean meat and the narrow bed, I will
not have accumulated virtue. Still
drifts feather the entrance to the park.
The birthday is eleven hours old.

VII

The birthday is eleven hours old.
The novelists' two sweet-stained daughters play
Camps under the kitchen stairs. Today,
hardly anything is bought or sold.
Hardly anybody eats alone.
Almost no trains run. Almost-suicides
and almost-murders lie in rows outside
the noisy quondam operating-room
where an exhausted intern, twenty-three
years old, mops up and sews. The children sing
below our gossip. Roast and fruit and wine
and smoke mix in the air near dinnertime.
The guests file foodwards while the darkening
sun of the dark solstice descends the tree.

ACKNOWLEDGMENTS

Harper & Row, Publishers, Inc.: "Elegy for Janis Joplin" and "Untoward Occurrence at Embassy Poetry Reading" from *Bad Moon Rising*. Copyright © 1973 by Thomas M. Disch. By permission of Harper & Row, Publishers.

Ambit (British): "Alba: September," "Elegy for Janis Joplin," "Later," "Sestina"
Antaeus: "Before the War"
Aphra: "She Bitches about Boys"
Aquarius (British): "Attack on the Iron Coast"
Arx: "Aquatic Park: 1967," "The Navigators," Part I
The Carleton Miscellany: "The Osiris Complex"
City: "Lines on the Death of Mme. de Staël," "The Muses"
Defiance: "Before the War"
Epoch: "*Apologia pro opere suo*," "The Sea Coming Indoors"
Expatriate Review: "Concordances"
The Little Magazine: "Iceplants," "Imaginary Translations," I and II, "The King of Cups Reversed," "Presentation Piece"
London Magazine (British): "Elektra on Third Ave.," "Lines on the Death of Mme. de Staël," "Pornographic Poem," "Villanelle," "Waiting"
Man Root: "The Navigators"
The New American Review (now *The American Review*): "*Aube Provençale*," "*Crépuscule Provençale*," "For Elektra," "Nimue to Merlin," "Sisterhood," "To the Reader"
Outposts (British): "She Bitches about Boys"
Poetry: Chicago: "An Alexandrite Pendant for My Mother," "*Chanson de l'Enfant prodigue*"
Poetry Northwest: "Exiles," "Untoward Occurrence at Embassy Poetry Reading"
Priapus (British): "The Sea Coming Indoors"
Quark: "Landscape for Insurrection," "Nightsong"
Samphire (British): "Alba: August," "Forage Sestina," "Ruptured Friendships, or The High Cost of Keys"
The San Francisco Quarterly: "The Art of the Novel"

Second Aeon (British): "The Dark Twin," "Nightsong"
Stand (British): "Like Aschenbach in Arizona," "Imaginary Translation," III
Strange Faeces (British): "Concordances"
The Times Literary Supplement (British): "Rooms in Bloomsbury"
Vector: "Pornographic Poem"
The Washington Square Review: "The Dark Twin"
Workshop (British): "Imaginary Translations," I and II, "Cities," "From *The Old Reliable,*" "The King of Cups Reversed," "The Muses"
The World: "Alba: October," "She Bitches about Boys"